LANDSCAPE WITH CHAINSAW

Poetry

A Jump Start
The Revenant
After Ovid: New Metamorphoses
(co-edited with Michael Hofmann)

Fiction

The Silver Age
Three Evenings and Other Stories
The Siege and Other Stories

LANDSCAPE WITH CHAINSAW

James Lasdun

CAPE POETRY

Published by Jonathan Cape 2001

2 4 6 8 10 9 7 5 3 1

First published in Great Britain in 2001 by
Jonathan Cape
Random House, 20 Vauxhall Bridge Road,
London SW1V 2SA

Random House Australia (Pty) Limited
20 Alfred Street, Milsons Point, Sydney,
New South Wales 2061, Australia

Random House New Zealand Limited
18 Poland Road, Glenfield,
Auckland 10, New Zealand

Random House (Pty) Limited
Endulini, 5A Jubilee Road, Parktown 2193, South Africa

The Random House Group Limited Reg. No. 954009

A CIP catalogue record for this book
is available from the British Library

ISBN 0224 06107 0

Papers used by The Random House Group Limited are natural,
recyclable products made from wood grown in sustainable forests;
the manufacturing processes conform to the environmental
regulations of the country of origin

Typeset by Palimpsest Book Production Limited,
Polmont, Stirlingshire
Printed and bound in Great Britain by
Creative Print and Design (Wales), Ebbw Vale

for Chris Shaw and Martha Kearney

CONTENTS

ACKNOWLEDGMENTS

London Review of Books, *New Writing 9* (Vintage), *New Yorker*, *New York Review of Books*, *Paris Review*, *Poetry Review*, *Times Literary Supplement*, *TriQuarterly*, *Yale Review*.

'Locals' won first prize in the 1999 *Times Literary Supplement*/Blackwells Poetry Competition.

I would like to thank the John Simon Guggenheim Memorial Foundation for their generous support.

ACKNOWLEDGMENTS

LOCALS

They peopled landscapes casually like trees,
being there richly, never having gone there,
and whether clanning in cities or village-thin stands
were reticent as trees with those not born there,
and their fate, like trees, was seldom in their hands.

Others to them were always one of two
evils: the colonist or refugee.
They stared back, half-disdaining us, half-fearing;
inferring from our looks their destiny
as preservation or as clearing.

I envied them. To be local was to know
which team to support: the local team;
where to drop in for a pint with mates: the local;
best of all to feel by birthright welcome
anywhere; be everywhere a local . . .

Bedouin-Brython-Algonquins; always there
before you; the original prior claim
that made your being anywhere intrusive.
There, doubtless, in Eden before Adam
wiped them out and settled in with Eve.

Whether at home or away, whether kids
playing or saying what they wanted,
or adults chatting, waiting for a bus,
or, in their well-tended graves, the contented dead,
there were always locals, and they were never us.

AMERICAN MOUNTAIN

I

Our Queen's English accents
kept the class-conscious English masses
at bay, while our looks and name
did the same for the upper classes.

Being there,
as opposed to just stopping by,
was a matter of what you arrived too late
to arrange: your ancestry.

'We're not English' went the family saying.
What were we then? We'd lopped
our branch off from the family tree:
anglophone Russian-German apostate Jews

mouthing Anglican hymns at church
till we renounced that too . . . Self-knowledge
was knowledge of not being this or this or this.
We were like stencils: our inverse had the edge

over whatever it was we were,
not that that would have mattered had I not
happened not to enjoy that throttling
knot of annulled speech gathering in my throat,

or the sense of not being in a room
I hadn't left, or being too light
to plant my feet. I was my opposite;
I chased myself across the planet

till I vanished through the looking glass
of the Atlantic Ocean
and woke up clinging to the tilted
patchwork of an American mountain.

II *A FAMILY TREE*

The locals,
Esopus Algonquins,
having already been massacred,
there's no-one with greater claims to an acre

than you have. As for your ancestry, it's yours
to choose from whoever cleared a spot
anywhere on these tough-fibred slopes and hollows.
Patent your own coat-of-arms – why not?

Elect your forbears from the pitch-brewers,
colliers, tanbark-peelers, the German
smelters at DeZeng's forge hammering molten
pigs of primordial bog-iron; shingle-splitters,

Dutch buckwheat farmers
who felled a white pine to pitch their claim,
cleared the land, then when the tree
rotted, had them a home;

apostate royalists who took 'The Test';
I have it by heart: *I the Subscriber*
Do most solemnly swear
that I renounce all allegiance to the King of Great Britain . . .

Take your pick, you'll know them
by what they left behind –
great bluestone dolmens the Irish quarrymen
cut and hauled down ice-roads, then abandoned;

abandoned orchards from Prohibition
when a backwoodsman could stay afloat
on twenty barrels of hard cider,
his knobbled trees still cranking out squint fruit;

abandoned houses – middle-income,
cathedral-ceilinged, faux post-and-beam
'Woodstock Contemporaries'
dotted along the creeks for IBM

before they downsized; abandoned grist-mills, graveyards
(and what landscape isn't finally the sum
of others' abandoned efforts to turn it
into themselves? Only the too tame

or the impossibly wild . . .)
As for my own family tree, I'd gladly
grandfather-in our predecessors
here on this slope of the mountain: glassblowers,

Bohemians mostly, shipped over
between the Embargo boom and the peacetime crash
– a brief, bright window –
to couple the virgin forests of Keefe Hollow

with the sands of Cooper Lake.
I see them at the glory hole
in their leather aprons and masks,
emptying their strong lungs

into the shimmering lungs of glass . . .
Choristers, fiddlers, jugglers,
with a taste for the gaudy,
they left behind almost nothing –

a few glass whimsies: dippers, turtles and canes;
bits of glass slag gleaming in the dirt,
and a marginal local
increase in transparency.

III *AFTER HEIDEGGER*

Lichtung: a clearing;
fire-break or beaver meadow,
Dutch farmer-pioneer meadows, stump-littered and raw;
first harvest ashes; second, Indian corn
tilled with a thorn-bush harrow.

'A man was famous'
the psalm reports, 'according
as he had lifted up axes upon thick trees'.
The trees are still thick, and although you've traded
that king for the secret king

of thought, and exchanged
your axe for a Makita,
it remains a matter of the ground beneath you; first
making it *unverborgen*: unconcealed,
then second, planting your feet.

I've muddled it all
like the old-time dairy-men
in their doggerel of gable and salt-box, their pastures
a garble of ditches. But that's how it is
after *Verfall*. The fallen

tend to a certain
makeshift approach towards life.
Like Kant they know nothing straight has ever been built
from the crooked timber of humanity,
and just keep patching the roof.

Theirs is the kingdom
of God, or at any rate
Dasein. Being here's just a question of having been
elsewhere unhappily long enough to feel
that that was exile, this not.

ADAM

Seed-hoarder: tipping his paper pouches
in unnibbleable coffers; fencing,
filching our food, homeland; won't chatter
the local woods brogue of chirrup and chuck,
his othering tongue unchristening tree,
unrocking rock.

He's not one of us; he's
definitely not one of us:
unstriped meat-breather pissing ammonia; we feign
blitheness but from each
brush-pile, oak-stump, ash-limb,
we are watching him.

EVE

I like that room,
the warm one with the machines
where the woman folds her shed skins.

I hang in the broken ceiling, watching her,
barely distinguishable
from the cold water pipe
and the coiled power cable.

I watch her all winter:
her long-legged hands,
the glinting needles of fur at her nape,
her red warmness
drifting in mammaly billows.

And now I show myself;
pour my flickering head
into her sac of air,
and slowly, willed against her own will,
her face rises like a rising moon,
opening palely to mine,

and in the wide O's of her eyes,
I see myself: my head like a big cut jewel,
the little watch-jewels of my eyes, yes,
my tongue the alive nerve of a rock,
and I feel her want,
a yearning almost,
as though for something already about to be lost,

and I offer myself.

RETURNING THE GIFT

for Nicholas Jenkins

For my birthday
my wife gives me a chainsaw;
a shiny blue Makita,
big as our child, heavy

as an impacted planet.
On every part of its body the makers
have slapped red warning stickers:
Stop! Danger of Death! Do Not Operate

Unless Experienced! The manual
elaborates: kickback,
where the blade bucks back through your neck;
blinding by woodchip or exploding fuel,

death by misguided tree-fall, tissue necrosis
from the engine vibrations . . . I look at my wife,
wondering what it means for a woman to give
her husband a gift such as this . . .

You said we needed one, remember?
She smiles, and it's true;
we're losing our meadow
to red maple, alder, poplar.

But the warnings . . . **Do Not Operate**
Unless Experienced! . . . For two weeks
I leave it untouched in its box,
then when I take it out,

A feeling of fear sinks through me:
must I deliberately rouse this murderous gift,
cradle its killing shaft
between my soft arms and belly,

carry it up where the old dairy pasture begins,
where the poplars loom sixty feet tall
with a sixty-foot will not to fall,
and plunge it into their skins?

*

Stripmall country: the chain
molecule of a shingled cinderblock cube
polymerised into hojo's, jiffy lube,
Walmart, K-Mart, and – where we're headed – Miron:

Museum of the American Present,
where can-do meets do-it-yourself,
where you can grab a dump-truck off the shelf
or a family-size nuclear power plant.

The chainsaw section's
display looks like a butcher's stall
selling various types of crocodile:
Makita, Husqvarna, Poulan . . . Thick festoons

of chainblade glitter rawly.
I hand my gift to the salesman,
a bearded giant, letting my wife explain.
As she talks, a glint comes into his eye:

Afraid? Afraid of what? Getting hurt?
He won't if he's in a right relation. Listen –
He leans toward me with a twinkling grin,
Molson-muscle swelling his green plaid shirt –

British, right? I nod. That question here
puts my guard up, like *are you Jewish?* did
in England where it meant *so you're a yid*,
at least to my hypersensitive ear,

as *British* here means – but I'm being paranoid;
he's got some other axe to grind: *King Arthur . . .*
Now there was a male mother,
nourishing his men on his own blood,

know what I'm saying? I don't. *Sir Bors, Gawain . . .*
The warrior's gone dead in the modern male . . .
I signal my wife *let's go*, to no avail:
Your wild man's hurting . . . I can feel his pain . . .

Old stags like me can help young bucks like you –
and it dawns on me I'm hearing
something I might have heard in a drum-filled clearing
on Bill Moyers, ten years ago –

How about I show you how to use it;
stop by your place some morning? I'd be glad to.
You could cut my – I cut him off: *No thank you*,
and turn, leaving the chainsaw. *Wait one minute!*

I'll make you a deal:
take the saw home for free;
buck some blowdowns before you drop a tree.
Live with it, let it settle, get a feel;

keep it a year, then if you want it, pay –
you'll know where to find me – if not, fine.
I'm doing this for your sake, son, not mine –
I'm starting to feel trapped . . . *I can't*, I bray,

I'm sick . . . I have this . . . deepdown . . . clumsiness . . .
cellular doggerel . . . my adolescence
was one long chapter of accidents –
this finger pruned by a door, the rest all thumbs,

my left arm propellor-chopped like sushi;
see? The world was my banana skin.
I cracked my collarbone on a trampoline.
I caught dysentery from a bottle of Vichy.

In the birthing room, when the nurse
gave me the clippers, it took me
not one snip, not two, but three
to cut our child's umbilicus.

Besides, I don't approve of cutting trees;
bad for the planet, don't you know? He nods:
Problem is, if you don't clear your woods,
they'll sure as hell clear you. That's how it is

here in America. Maybe where you're from
you get to live as if that wasn't so;
as if your needs all balanced long ago
and everything fits snugly in its home,

but things aren't like that here. We still need teeth,
and not to bite our nails, as I see you do.
Either you clear your woods or they'll clear you –
You said that! Listen: I'm afraid of death,

or, to be more exact, of my apparent
death-wish, or more accurate still,
my possibly damaged, definitely faltering will
to stay alive: each lapse an 'accident'.

That's all there is to say, except goodbye.
But as I turn again, he grabs my wife
who half seems to expect it: *tell him, Eve;*
you gave it to him, now you tell him why!

★

Instead of an apple, the tree
grew a ripe chainsaw:
a shiny blue Makita.
The woman plucked it and gave it to me.

Since then I have cut through a number of things:
a stand of maple and an acre of alder,
several chips on my shoulder,
the mother of all apron strings . . .

On every part of its body, the maker
had slapped red warnings: **Stop!**
Danger of Death! I took it up
to the edge of our once-clear

mountain meadow,
and where the woods had jumped the stone wall,
and a blossoming red maple
stood waving at its own shadow,

I set the throttle and choke,
yanked the starter cord:
once, twice, three times, hard as I could,
and my dubious gift awoke.

VAN MAANAN'S STAR

The Coulter telescope, a wedding gift,
stands unused in the barn, its trunk-thick,
man-high, scarlet, cardboard tube
wrapped in black plastic.
Six years of marriage and not one night
out in the field as they'd planned, adrift
in magnified starlight.

They've lain out there at night but not for this;
not yet: the unmown summer clover's
featherbed too soft for any
still unblunted lovers
to lie on, stargazing. So there it looms,
slumbering like an unmoved chesspiece
or a mausoleum's

sealed treasure waiting for the afterlife;
for surely not till then will they find
leisure for this or the rest:
the dimly outlined
yearnings a bench-press, skis, smoke-oven –
all the junk the acquisitive
impulse love now and then

mistook itself for – accumulated
there in that big-bellied Catskill barn.
And that's as it should be: love,
work, a home, children
at full spate in their lives now, hurtling them
too fast forward for any look but ahead;
arms full or cup abrim

whichever . . . And if there's any blessing
other than its shine a star can shed,
it's this: that that dozing
eye remain lidded
forever, or at least till what they see
is what burned here the nights they lay down there
burning as brightly.

CHAINSAW I

As though you held in your hands
the severed head of Orpheus
crying his own *sparagmos*;
the mutilated bower
falling, still in flower—

or your own split kingdom's
hybrid of lion and unicorn:
at once dismembering tooth
and clarifying horn.

APOSTASY

Literally 'standing off'.
Standoffishness, then.
The outsider's version of snobbery,
in our case amplified,
us being doubly outside.

Our car, for instance, a Citröen Safari,
unassimilable among the Fords and Austins
of the Sussex highways,
was all curving proboscis,
with an otherworldly hiss

as it rose on its air-suspension
like a beast from the Cabala.
They were so rare in those days, owners
saluted each other on the road.
Not us though;

our idea of a club
was what, having first excluded
most of the rest of the world,
you then proceeded to snub.
Something you joined by dismemberment.

I recall this as I stand,
the flower of chivalry,
in my visored orange helmet and blue nylon chaps,
idling chainsaw in hand,
by a flowering red maple.

BULLION

Muscled word
like stallion or billion;
a bull crossed with a lion,
its sound a roil or *bouillon*
of molten, masculine gold.

Falling knives on the Dow;
my money-soul poor-mouthing,
writhing;
Fathers, fill me
with the word of gold . . .

Now that it pays to have them,
I'm praying for an ancestor
with the bad luck and teeth
to have emptied a mouthful of gold
into a Bern-bound ingot.

I think of Daniel,
another *déraciné*,
his strength all weakness, negation;
the kind of man who dims light-bulbs,
who sets your teeth on edge

with his dreams of his own teeth crumbling.
He saw a beast in a vision:
dreadful and terrible and strong exceedingly;
and it had great iron teeth:
it devoured and brake in pieces . . .

The lions wouldn't touch him.
He wasn't kosher;
toxic with anti-matter:
one drop of his blood would drown them
like gold in sea-water.

My own teeth
have mercury fillings;
a recipe for erethism –
my lassitude;
my hebetude . . .

DEATHMEADOW MOUNTAIN

Celan's
meeting with Heidegger:
by John Felstiner's account
an impasse or non-event,
like Daniel's meeting with the lions;

the walk
through the blossoming Black
Forest broken off – too wet;
the visit to the dark hut
(like a negative of Goethe's oak

unfelled
out of respect in the
otherwise clearcut meadows
of Buchenwald, as Resnais's
Night and Fog had disclosed – 'they build

the camp',
Celan had translated,
'they respect the oak'); *Denker*
and *Dichter* pausing to drink
at the star-topped well – less well than sump;

its throat
black with 'deathbringing speech';
the tongue of Being . . . its bitter
waters black as the water
Moses had to cleanse with his snake-rod;

the star
glittering in its depths
like a dove in a cat's eye,
and the book, *das Buch*, in the
hut in the *Waldwasen*, signed there

in hope
of a 'word in the heart'
from the Secret King of Thought,
the *Meister*, who withheld it
till the poet gave up.

PATROL CAR, BEAR MOUNTAIN

I

Starting back late from the ridge
I lost the path and scrambled
down through a gully of fern and fat-budded
mountain laurel. A disused quarry
dropped from the knobbled claw of an oak
looped by a hawser decades had embedded
so deeply in its girth two swollen
lips had formed as if the tree
were swallowing back its own umbilicus
of twisted steel. I gripped the cable
and lowered myself down. A mound of shale
breasted the shadows below, and under that
the car; a sheriff's patrol car,
not on a road, not on any trail
or vestige of a trail I could make out,
but there, vibrantly, its stalled
shock of metals inexplicable, and there,
glimmer-patched under his windshield, the uniformed
figure at the wheel, just staring forward.

II

Familiar
whiff of the old id-slum:
those disembodied
lips and talons, that stone breast mapping
an all-but-forgotten hebdomad
of the spirit, where to be dropping
anxiously was to be going home.

Cop in the woods
I've found you, or have you
found me? I'd vectored
something intruded, anomalous
around here (then instantly blocked it);
something afield, shall we say,
from its legitimate purview.

Not how but when
you got here's the one truth
I'd care enough – oh,
but you've been here forever of course,
mother-of-all-fathers, haven't you,
with your book and billy club,
risen up out of the klippoth?

Demiurge sunk
so deeply in my own
acre, at this point
you're almost less curb or fifth column
than double or quadruple agent
or at least a familiar
if stony shoulder to cry on.

Should I approach?
I can't. Something's crabbing
my footsteps sideways
even as I point them towards you,
as though a glass wall – but it's not glass,
it's time: harder if almost
as see-through. Behind it, sobbing,

a kid's ghost-face
in a bracken of dreads,
and I'm out of here;
I've seen too much already, the leaves
blackening around you almost faster
than I can move, the wind cold,
the laurel blossoms dead in their buds.

THE APOSTATE

The mirror was oval like her face.
Almond eyes, the blue-black curls
an equivocal admirer
once plied his fingers through
wistfully, before letting go.

Outside, hedgerows glittered;
rosehips, ripening cobnuts,
stitched in like silk as if the county
had slid from a palace wall and settled there.
Why do I long to be here when I am here?

The church battens onto its hill . . . Inside
eyes found her, lingered furtively
as on a curving surface that reflected
subtly distorted images of themselves,
and in their fascination felt a fear:

would she dissolve in them or they in her?
Too much brimmed in her presence;
the convert's accusing innocence,
betrayal's incandescence,
as if in her gesture the abandoned scrolls

had spilt themselves in one self-immolating
flash of outrage. Everything felt it –
lectern, pulpit; surely the anxious
altar would sprout and buckle into a star,
Cranmer's prayerbook open onto a *Sh'ma*!

Herself, she felt their looks as an unclothing;
a difficult, necessary dream
of intimate exposure to a crowd
flaying her strangeness from her till she stood
naked, at once their victim and one of them.

Kneeling, she closed her eyes and prayed –
What is this burden that grows
heavier the more of it I shed?
Here is the vicar. His pink face
pokes from its white fallopian flower

glossy as a hatchling angel.
He warbles like a dove. Exotic Anglican
incense of lilies, willow, wavering reeds
purls through the rafters, thinly.
He lays the host out like a picnic tea.

She takes her place . . . Impossible
not to feel for once the word made flesh,
watching her kneel and drink . . .
It splinters through her.
Out in the jangling air

she feels invisible, dispersed,
as if the gold-lipped chalice
had swallowed her into itself;
into the iron and flagstones, the pitted pillars,
into the earth outside – and this is grace,

briefly: an unestrangement from the sunken
farmtracks bleached like vertebrae, the sour
haze of hop pollen, scarlet hunt
blotting into a field, the whites
of cricketers on the green

where Christ the umpire
smiles on an eternity
of Judasless elevens,
comfy in his floppy crucifix
of lambswool sweaters, his jolly crown of caps.

HOPS

When the drunk at the bar of the Royal Oak
glared into my face,
gripping his pint like a hand grenade
from which he'd just taken the pin,
and told me what he told me,

the pang I felt
was like the split that goes on riving
all the way down the trunk
from one sound blow to the wedge,
as though it had been there forever, waiting.

That was the last time I felt at home
in a country pub, therefore England;
that, for me, being England –
that badger-set gloom
with its little church organ of bottles and pumps,

where a dim light from the sconce lamps
tools the unfakeable ease
on figures who belong there,
simply, set on their stools like chessmen,
as calmly set in their ways,

while over the burrowy stalings of pipe-smoke, yeast,
ancestral piss from the Gents
flares the bitter, freshening smell of hops,
feudal and vital; the inexhaustible gold dust
of the true Anglican host.

I worked on the neighboring farm one summer,
hop-picking with a crew of gypsies.
the twelve-acre pole-and-wire trellises,
diagrammatic in spring,
had spurted their vines:

ten thousand living maypoles
in a haze of hop dust.
We hacked our way down the rows,
bundling tangled armfuls
into the stripping and sorting machines.

The clustering bracts
were sticky as flypaper:
little papery pouches of yellow snuff.
We stuffed them into burlap sacks,
then hauled them off to the ovens.

Two weeks into the season
the head-dazing, sour-gold smell
was in us like our own spoor;
we moved through the drifts of late summer
sweating it like the musk of hop gods.

We were the gods of that place if anyone was –
the stubble-gold shire streaming through us;
in sleep, crashed out under oak trees,
our sticky hands still sorting
the gold-filled, bunched, shrunken heads –

Albion juju;
I was full of it then:
Malory, Holinshed,
King John's sunk ducats
sifting from gold to sand

to hop pollen . . .
I'm exorcising it now
with a backwoods ghost-fragrance
of birch beer and applejack
on a barn porch under black locusts

where thumb-sized hummingbirds
zoom through the crimson bee-balm
and whenever I move my pen
a fountain of goldfinches
splashes out of the bushes.

A TIE-DYE T-SHIRT

Home from prep school
in my short-trousered herringbone suit,
I counted hippies on the streets of Notting Hill.
In their crushed-velvet bell-bottoms
they moved like shaggy-hooved centaurs.
I tagged along with a group
drifting down the Portobello.
One of them, tall and slim with long black hair,
wore a tie-dye T-shirt;
the first I had ever seen:
yellow mainly, with starbursts of rose and lime-green.
He was playing a silver flute. I felt myself
in the presence of superior beings,
as Major Wynkoop said of the Cheyennes.

Now thirty years later
my daughter makes me a tie-dye T-shirt
from one of the kits they sell
in the kitschy Tinker Street head-shops.
I put it on and a strange
tremor of happiness goes through me.
I've half a mind to crack open
one of the spiked pods on this Jimson Weed,
toss its seed-spurt into the air,
swallow what the gods let me catch,
and hallucinate a week or two
in the psychedelic spring meadow,
where goldfinches and rose-breasted grosbeaks
flit between the creamy shadblow
and the lime-green,
catkin-veiled birches.

BLACK LOCUST GROVE

for Jonathan Nossiter

Shallow-rooted like us,
less colonists than refugees,
they crowd into spent farmland,
twisting to find the light,
eking out thin livings; ghetto trees,

branchless till they crown, sparsely;
all thrift against the summer foliage,
swaying in ghostlike plumes as if our grave
forefathers had come back to observe us
working beneath them on the porch.

Named for a desert scourge
their pods are said to resemble,
they press their kinship through our own names;
our strangeness in the Anglo-Saxon forest
of Smiths and Browns ours clashed with every roll-call.

(Homework: invent your family's crest;
maybe you never had to but I did:
a dun-colored lass – what else? The class tittered.
Later I invented my family's psychology:
Anglo, Super-Anglo and Yid.)

A diet of dust and stones. But that's behind us,
isn't it? Sweetened to milk and honey . . .
Though whatever complicity
we aspire to with these black locusts,
it isn't that their leaves turn out to be money,

but their pure obduracy, their rock-smooth
rings like agate rings, so hard the wood
won't rot or even soften when it's dead
but sparks against the chainsaw blade
and burns too hot for comfort in the woodstove.

THE BACKHOE

for Pia

Van Kleef had plowed the road, we'd cut a track
from the woodpile to the door, dug out the car,
shovelled where the hemlocks shook their sleeves
in thudding dollops on the ice-swollen eaves.
The yard was like a building site or boneyard:
a rubble of knuckles and skulls; we stood there,
the city couple, patting ourselves on the back
when the first heavy flakes of the second blizzard

came drifting in. And now all over again
things swell and soften. The grey debris
brightens, loses its edge in a luminous
myopic blur; a velvet of spectral moss,
as in some lush, sub-zero planet's scheme
for rot, spreads over the woodpile; every tree
ridges its branches with a thick white vein,
and after its brief thaw blankness's regime

clamps down again. This time it looks conclusive;
more scrupulous than before, the flakes
falling so fast a thick white darkness
blots the windows and a steady hiss
chafes at the hush: white noise . . . What can we do
but sit and watch ourselves vanish like two mistakes
under the white-out brush? And now Van Kleef
calls up to say the snowplow can't get through;

'You'll have to wait for the backhoe. Don't know when –'
and the line goes dead.
                              Two days later. The sky's
been blue since then, dead calm,

as if it knew exactly how much harm
was necessary for our object lesson
in our own helplessness, and bore no actual malice,
except that the power's out too, that the pipes have frozen,
that seven blankets are seven times colder than one,

that the world outside's like the sea of glass
in Revelation: deadlocked, the only motion
hemlock shadows inching over the snow
and the apocalyptic glow –
jacinth, beryl, chrysolite –
spilling out from the clouds as the afternoon
swerves into evening . . . Hadn't we reached this impasse
somewhere before? Silence, the numbing white

solidified future pressing in,
doors out heavy as boulders at a tomb:
terminal blockage, ourselves
cooling like statues as though our lives
had parted already and moved on elsewhere
without us . . . We'd waited for the end to come
but it hadn't! And I think of what happened then
now, as a rumbling wakes us and we stare

out through the window, not quite sure
what a backhoe is, and even when it passes
not much the wiser; the house-high
cablights piercing in too blindingly
to make out more than its force and dazzle,
snow splitting like the sea in front of Moses
in two tall glittering plumes, the blacktop's raw
glisten ribboning back out over the hill.

BLUESTONE

for Michael Hofmann

After the glassworks failed and the dairy farms,
battening onto the shrapnel tracts
clearcut for the furnace, failed in turn,
and the last resort gave up its empty rooms
to chipmunks and rattlesnakes, the facts
dampened all but the simplest dreams:
scraping a living; tending a bit of garden.

I didn't think I'd like it but I did,
inexplicably, this neither soothing
nor somehow uplifting landscape
of wooded bluestone crags crannied
by hollows and gullies, where nothing
human ever quite flourishes or quite
abandons – as it doubtless should – all hope.

Pecoy Notch, Bear Mountain, Sugarloaf;
each a begrudging mother's stony teat
yielding nothing not strictly needed
and not everything that is: not love,
at best a vaguely nutritive sweat
on which her stonier offspring vaguely thrive:
stones best of all; black locusts that look dead

most of the year, then when they are won't fall
but stiffen to thin flint pillars; ironwood;
unrottable tamarack; spiky, rock-solid pear trees;
anything barbed or thorned, any animal
or for that matter human, less flesh and blood
than tooth or talon, bristle, antler or quill . . .
Porcupines abound, wild turkeys

clatter in droves, briefly turning the bluestone
into themselves. I see it less as landscape
than as the image of a residuum:
clean-etched, irreducible unillusion;
hard to like, harder to give up;
the durable part of pleasure, living on
after its acid-bath in boredom.

BETWEEN A AND B

The Tree of Heaven's lost its winter bloom
of plastic bags. The leaves are coming out –
a fizz of reddish green afloat
over the garbage it sprouted from.
You wonder why it bothers. Hasn't it heard
nobody's interested in that kind of thing . . . ?
A memory: six or seven, visiting
a dying uncle. Cocked against his sickbed
I flashed my new Swiss Army knife, and fanned
the blades, grinning, as if I'd hauled that shine
out from some pristine darkness of my own.
'What do you want to show me such things for?'
he muttered. I was hurt! I'd thought the gesture
would please him. I begin to understand.

CHAINSAW II

Gesang ist Dasein (Rilke)

and given the little caring left to care
for the possibly even less worth caring for;
given how at any given moment
you or anyway I would probably rather

be doing nothing than what we're doing,
this at least has the merit
not just of drowning out the drone
of Being's involuntary effort not to drown

in Nothingness, but also
of bringing things back to first principles:
the need to carve out a niche for ourselves;
our singular relation to what we love.

And if song is existence,
one could do worse for the roar
of life being lived to the hilt
than a blade plunged in solid wood.

PROPERTY: THE BEAR

The little birches battle through the gravel.
When they come out, if they do, they're strong;
straight-stemmed in a globe of buds, withholding
nothing of themselves. And the pumpkin vines,
shooting zigzags of leaves along
like scabbard chasings, in clean-etched lines,
brim at their formal bounds, as if unfolding

more than just their substance;
a presence, if you like, or an assertion.
Later, counter-assertions: gypsy moths
fretting moth-sized holes in the birch leaves; wild
turkey hatchlings, twitchy with caution,
pecking the unripe pumpkins . . . Build
anything, let alone Rome, and you conjure Goths

instantly, or is it you that's the Goth?
Whichever . . . You either bang your drum –
be it Circus, Talking or Lambeg –
or else make way for a louder drummer.
The saintliest wisdom may be playing dumb
but being dead's dead quiet and nothing's dumber,
besides which one man's saint is another man's scumbag . . .

Slug-bitten radishes, crabgrass on the field drain,
carpenter ants in the barn, a blow-hard
Highway Superintendent who wants to pave
the dirt road which you like the way it is;
volunteer maples filing into the yard . . .
Living is possibly nothing more than this;
who, at any rate, wouldn't feel more alive

wielding, let's say, a chainsaw than a seed-drill?
Whose dreams are too unfallen to come to rest
on one tree's toppling crash with greater glee
than a whole forest's daily tonnage of wood
dredged from the dirt? No-one except a forest.
An ant would use a chainsaw if it could.
So would a slug. So, I suspect, would a tree.

All the more strange then, to stand
in the small hours one summer,
after a month of drought, roused by the din
of a ribbed aluminum can being burst
on a jag of granite, and watch the bear –
a swale of glittering blackness – half-immersed
in its spilt trove of birdseed, tucking in,

leisurely, undisturbed by us,
swaying on the anchor of his head
like a big ship or sunken constellation;
to watch, and feel for once like letting go –
not just the forty-odd pounds of black-oil seed
but everything got, bought, garrisoned, as though
defencelessness against this visitation

had made it almost welcome . . . He finishes,
then looms up at the kitchen screen –
all that divides us – peering in for the trash
he's caught a whiff of; and it's almost sweet –
like an immense good nature breaking in –
to watch the frail screen bulging where he probes it,
then four long claws come slashing through the mesh.

BIRCH TREE WITH CHAINSAW

for Pia

Five months; five cords of hardwood;
ash mostly, hickory, oak;
greying in the weather,
by April starting to rot,
outsides sodden by May,
too crumbly even to splinter.

But then to uncover the first layer:
white birch, bright with the whiteness
that whitens your hands like chalk;
flesh-colored wood still firm
in its sheath of papery bands,
flaw-lined like slubbed silk.

Five months . . . Our pilgrim winter
in the squalls of parenthood,
the money-storms of ownership;
hodding the muddy ruins of the woodpile –
fungus-gilled, webby with slimes –
load by load to the stove,

till I come to the layer of white birch;
dust-white, the bark still tight,
sparkling in its pin-shoal,
the logs so sprung a knock
all but sets them ringing on their rails
like blocks on a glockenspiel.

I remember it; my first
plunge-cut, the bellying trunk
too plump for the usual felling kerf,
a bride among her bridesmaids
in its copse of lithe saplings.
I plunged the blade in, circling till she gave . . .

Now five cords later, to exhume
these limbs again, the winter-rotted
burial rags and pulp all gone;
just these in their bone-bright dazzle
as though to remind us we'd left
something unruined or still to ruin.

I feed them into the fire,
glad of its brightening glass
as they loosen their storm of flames,
and I'm seeing it again
veining the blue air with its ore
in tangled, silver-white seams.

Before I cut it I touched the trunk
as if its belly might kick like yours –
remember? – thaw-pools glinting in the woods,
shadblows foaming, and there,
indestructible, leaning into the light,
The birch in its veil of buds.

LEO RISING

He doesn't believe in me.
His neighbor saw me here on the ridge,
but he doesn't believe his neighbor.
I watch him from my bluestone ledge

hacking blueberry scrub with a whetted scythe,
clearing red maples with a chainsaw
in his tie-dye T-shirt.
I watch him as the King of Sicilia

watches the King of Bohemia
or Koba watches Lev Bronstein,
and I step from my bluestone ledge
to my ledge of blue sky,

and I watch him
venturing an existence,
presuming to continue to exist,
and I put on my brazen glance,

my long knives and my brownshirt,
my coat of napalm,
my tank-pack of Agent Orange,
and I watch him

clearing his wilderness, watering
the deserts of Bohemia,
perpetuating the affront of his existence
in the rainbowy flim of his T-shirt,

and his unbelief calls me forth
in midsummer, in the month of Av,
and I enter
fruit, flower and leaf,

and I disclose myself:
a catastrophe of golds;
a drought-napped, bracken-maned
torrent of dry blades.

WOODSTOCK

Wudestoc: a clearing in the woods.
Forty miles from the town itself;
the name, as in Herzl's *Judenstaat*,
less about place than disclosure –
of a people, or an idea.

I was at prep school in Surrey at the time,
pre-pubescent; under my yearning eyes,
the grounds – all greensward with copper beeches –
glimmered like the veil of heaven
about to be torn open.

At noon we stood on parade in divisions
and marched into lunch like soldiers.
The dining room
was painted with scenes from King Arthur.
Vividly out of green water a naked arm

held a great shining sword . . .
In my first wet dream
Queen Guinevere seduced me in her tent.
There was an initiation rite:
six boys scragged you on the stony puntabout.

You were terrified but you wanted it.
Thereafter one had trouble with one's pronouns.
I found Queen Guinevere in the bed to my left.
Her name was Richard, I think, or Robert;
a cavalier to my roundhead,

or as one goy put it,
my jewnicorn.
Nightly my left arm crept between her sheets,
sneaking home in the small hours,
sticky with Guinevere's flowers.

We were like South Sea Islanders,
worshipping existence from afar
with our own cargo-cult
of whatever beached on our shore.
One boy found the empty sleeve

of Electric Ladyland.
We gazed till we felt the heavens opened
and the spirit like a dove descending:
Jimi and twenty-one naked girls,
Guineveres to a man;

Jimi in a braided military coat
and flower-power shirt;
a hawk-taloned dove
late of the 101st Airborne,
mouthing our cry of love.

I signed up for classical guitar
and plucked a lute-gentle twelve-bar blues
at our all-boys disco night
where the nursing sister briefly graced us,
sending her thanks and kisses on scented paper

which, in our excitement, we tore to pieces.
Later I bought an electric, though by that time
my left arm was half-numb
and the best people, Jimi included,
had checked out of the stadium.

I'm in Woodstock now,
on a mountain clearing,
my own *lichtung*
or niche in existence,
watching old footage of Woodstock.

Peace and Love . . . and War:
The throbbing choppers ferrying musicians
over the refugee traffic,
over the city-sized singalong
of Country Joe's 'What are we fighting for?'

Pete Townsend in white jeans and braces
like one of Kubrick's droogies,
beating up his own axe;
Joe Cocker playing air-guitar, or is it
air-chainsaw, or air-bazooka?

Had I not seen this in a vision?
That record sleeve my tab of pure Owlsley:
vividly out of the lake the women rising,
bare-breasted, flower-strewn, Guineveres to a man;
Kesey's yippies frolicking in the mud –

A Mesopotamian puntabout;
Wavy Gravy offering to feed the multitude,
addressing them 'listen, man . . .'
Too much already!
And after Max Yasgur's blessing,

Hendrix, amused-looking, laconic,
as in his Dick Cavett interview –
Cavett: 'are you disciplined, do you
get up every morning and work?' And Jimi:
'well, I try to get up every morning . . .'

48

The long fringes on his sleeve
make eagle-wings as he sharpens his axe,
the usual left-handed Fender,
with its phallic arm
and womanly curves.

It was at Monterey, not here,
that he set fire to it on stage
after dry-humping an amp;
his instinct for sacrifice narrowing in
like Adam's in the Talmud,

his axe the *re'em* or one-horned ox
— a jewnicorn —
offered up to Jehovah.
I think of my left arm rising
vividly out of Lake Como,

slashed by a speedboat propeller
I'd summoned for the job
(of my hand didst thou require it)
of securing a right-handed future
righter-handed, that is,

which it did with the dexterity, ha-ha,
of a kosher butcher
removing the sciatic nerve
in honor of Jacob who lost his sciatic nerve
dry-humping an angel.

The water foamed red, red
as the mingling red chain-oil and flower-juices
of the blossoming red maples
I cleared from our meadow —
Guineveres to a man —

and vividly out of the water
the unsheathed sword of my own
startlingly white bone *And he said thy name*
between two labial flesh-flaps
shall no longer be called Jacob . . .

But Jimi, who still later could be said
to have offered up his own head
that we not forget to remember
the art not of getting somewhere
but of being there,

is in mellower fettle here. Calmly
he sharpens his curved axe
Quat! hit clatered in the clyff
for a few bursts of Machine Gun,
bringing the torso to his teeth,

a panther devouring a fawn,
our eagle-clawed dove;
then with the dexterity
of a kosher *shohet,*
or Saladin with King Richard's handkerchief,

or Sir Bertilak blooding Sir Gawain,
proceeds to slash apart the Star-Spangled Banner,
bending the strings till they
carve through its flesh like the blades
(I will not let thee go except thou bless me)

of a speedboat propeller,
the bitten steel biting back
into his flesh, which is ours,
just as the Star-Spangled Banner
is the blood-spangled heavens torn open

for the spirit like an F-105 Thunderchief descending,
and the sound you hear is the sound
of something being annihilated
calmly, and for good;
and your name,

whatever it is,
is no longer what it was,
for as a prince
hast thou power with God and with men,
and hast prevailed.

HAPPY THE MAN

Goodbye words;
my faltering muse's
unevenly burning flame
has sputtered out, and now like Diocletian
I'm taking early retirement.

Homesteading:
goats, organic lettuce,
that's the project; and when I
buck blowdowns or shovel dung from a pickup,
I'll remember how you once

were all I
needed or anyway
wanted of the crack and grain
of real things; how in your loam they'd swell, split
and banner out into themselves . . .

Now you can
just be their names again:
bluestone, shiplap, whatever.
And if I write, it'll be with a seed-drill;
a quatrain of greens per bed, no sweat.

The dirt road
dead-ends on wilderness;
sometimes at night you can hear
unearthly gabblings: Bear Mountain's coyotes
closing in on a kill. Pure poetry.